MW01247435

JOEL'S GEMS

JOEL OSTEEN JOKES!

"2 Book Combo!"

Joel Osteen Jokes (Original)
and
Joel Osteen Jokes Version 2

By Don Pasco

http://ebooksworthreading.com

Other books by Don Pasco

JOEL'S GEMS

"Joel Osteen Quotes"

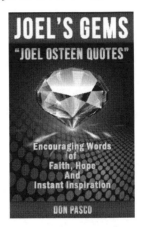

Name That Artist –

The Multiple Choice Music Celebrity Quiz Game

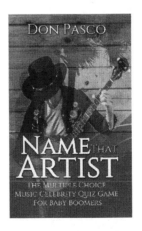

ISBN-13: 978-1517076450

ISBN-10: 1517076455

JOEL'S GEMS

"Joel Osteen Jokes"

(Original)

**Hilarious Collection
Of
Joel Osteen's
Funniest
Short, Clean Jokes**

Table of Contents

Free Bonuses

Joel Osteen Jokes (Video version)
Joel Osteen Jokes (Audio version)

For a limited time purchasers of Joel's Gems "Joel Osteen Jokes" can receive the audio book version AND the video version of the same title by visiting the page below. So if you would like to watch Joel deliver these jokes in his funny and entertaining way or just listen while doing something else, visit the URL below to claim your bonus.

http://donpasco.com/joel-osteen-jokes-video-free-bonus

Introduction

Every week Pastor Joel Osteen likes to get started with something funny. Having a sense of humor is an important attribute for all of us to have. We all need the capacity to laugh. After all, **joy is a gift from God.**

We all know there's more than enough negative things in the world that we hear about each and every day, either through the news media or even in our own lives and the lives of those around us.

Are You a Light Hearted Person?

I personally feel that we should always be looking for things that make us laugh, chuckle or smile. I like the feeling of being a "Light Hearted" person and I hope you do too.

1

I am arguably Joel Osteen's "biggest" fan but rather than argue about it, I'd prefer to just give in to anyone else who feels that they are a "bigger" fan than me. I currently weigh about 170 pounds so if you weigh more than I do, I guess you have a valid point.

Now if you found that (my corny joke) even slightly amusing, I believe that you are going to absolutely love this collection of Joel's Jokes that I have put together all in one place that you can read in one sitting if you'd like.

And if you're anything like me, **you'll enjoy telling them just as much as reading them.**

Joel states upfront that the jokes are not doctrinally correct... that they're just to make us laugh so I too want to mention that here.

Are you ready to get started?

Well then turn the page! LOL

No Really! Laugh OUT LOUD!

Chapter 1

Ladies Joel Heard About

I heard about this kindergarten teacher.
She wanted to teach her students about self esteem.

She said to her class "Everyone who thinks you are dumb, please stand up."

She didn't think anybody would stand
and she'd make the point
how no one was dumb.

But about that time little Jonny stood up.
She didn't quite know what to do.

She said,

"Now Johnny do you really think

that you're dumb?"

He said, "No Ma'am,

I just hate to see you standing there

All by yourself."

*****

I heard about this 85 year old woman.

She went on a blind date

with a 92 year old man.

She came home very frustrated

and her daughter said,

"Mom, what's wrong?"

She said, "I had to slap him three times."

The daughter said,

"You mean he tried to get fresh?"

She said, "No. I thought he was dead."

*****

This was sent to me (Joel)
from a senior citizen's home.

It's about this 84 year old woman.

She'd gotten out of shape and knew
she needed to start exercising.

So she decided to join
an aerobics class for seniors.

And the first day,
she bent and twisted
and gyrated back and forth,
jumped up and down,
perspired for over an hour.

But she said by the time
she got her leotards on
the class was over.

*****

I heard about this Mother, one Sunday morning she went into her son's bedroom and she said, "Son, wake up. It's time to go to church."

He kinda groaned and rolled over and said, "No Mom, I'm not going to church today."

She said, "What do you mean you're not going? Why not?"

He said, "Mom, I'll give you two good reasons. Number one, I don't like those people. And number two, they don't like me." She said, "Son, that's no excuse.

I'll give you two Better reasons why you SHOULD go. Number one, you're fifty-nine years old and number two, you're the Pastor."

*****

I heard about this kindergarten teacher.
She was walking around her classroom
as her students drew pictures.

She noticed this one little girl
drawing so intently
she asked her what she was drawing.

The little girl said she was
drawing a picture of God.

The teacher kind of laughed.
She said, "Oh Honey nobody really knows
what God looks like.

The little girl without missing a beat said,
"They will in a minute."

*****

I heard about this lady
that was shopping with her husband.

He had asked her to
not buy any new clothes.

Well she saw this dress in the window
and decided to try it on.

She liked it so much,
she bought it in secret.

Couple of days later
the husband discovered it
and he was so upset.

And she explained to him
that when she tried it on
it looked so good
that Satan tempted her to buy it
and she just couldn't resist it.

He said, "Well, why didn't you do
what the scripture says
and say "get behind me Satan?"

She said, "I did and he told me
it looked even better from a distance."

*****

I heard about this elderly lady.
She came into church one Sunday morning
and a friendly usher greeted her
and said, "Ma'am
where would you like to sit?"

She said, "I would like to sit
in the very front row."

And he said, "Oh no Ma'am,
you don't want to do that.
Our Pastor is very boring.
He'll put you to sleep.

Let me seat you somewhere else."

She was appalled.
She said, "Sir,
do you know who I am?"

He said, "no."

She said, "I am the Pastor's Mother."

He hung his head in embarrassment
and finally he looked up and said,
"Ma'am, do you know who I am."

She said, "no."
He said, "Thank God."

*****

Chapter 2

Men Joel Heard About

I heard about these three men
that were out hiking
through the wilderness.

They came upon this very violent,
raging river and they needed to
get to the other side.

The first man prayed
"Please God give me the strength
to make it across."

And POOF!

13

God gave him big arms and strong legs
and he was able to swim across in 2 hours.

Seeing this the next man said,
"God please give me the strength
and the tools
I need to make it across."

And POOF!
God gave him a boat.
He was able to row across in 30 minutes.

The next man said,
"God give me the strength,
the tools and the intelligence
to make it across."

And POOF!
God turned him into a woman.

She looked at the map,
hiked 5 minutes up stream
and then walked across the bridge.

*****

This was sent to me (Joel)
from a senior citizen's home.

It's about a 92 year old man.
He wasn't feeling well one day
and so he decided to go
to the doctor and have a check-up.

A few days later the doctor
saw him out walking down the street
with a beautiful young lady by his side.

And he seemed to be
just as happy as could be.

The Doctor was kind of surprised.
He said, "Wow you sure are
doing a lot better."

The man said, "Yes Doctor,
I just took your orders.

You said get a hot momma
and stay cheerful."

The Doctor said, "I didn't say that!
I said you got a heart murmur.
Be careful!"

*****

A man called the church office and said,
"Can I speak to
the head hog at the trough?"

The secretary was offended.

She said, "If you mean the Pastor
then you need to refer to him as
"The Pastor", but **you may not** call him
the head hog at the trough!"

The man said, "That's fine.
I was just planning on giving
$10,000 dollars to the building fund."

The lady replied, "Hold on.
Porky just walked in."

*****

I heard about this elderly man.
He'd had a serious hearing problem
for years and years.
He could hardly hear anything.

And one day he went to the doctor
and he was fitted with
a new type of hearing aid,
to where he could hear
one hundred percent.

A month later he went back
for a check up
and the doctor said,
"Man your family must really be happy.
Your hearing is perfect."

He said, "No, I haven't told my family.

I just sit around and listen to the conversations, and I've changed my will three times."

*****

I heard about this burglar
that broke into a home one night.

As he was stealing the stereo,
he heard a voice saying
"Jesus is watching you."

He froze in his tracks and he shined
the flashlight around the room.

And he saw a parrot over in the corner.
He said, "did you say that to me?"
The parrot said, "Yes,
I'm just trying to warn you."

He said, "warn me,
what are you talking about? Who are you?"
The parrot said, "My name is Moses."

The burglar laughed and said,
"What kind of crazy people
would name a parrot Moses?"

The parrot said, "the same kind of people that would name a One Hundred
and Fifty pound Rottweiler Jesus."

*****

I heard about this college professor,
he told his students he was going to
prove that there is no God.

He said, "God, if you're real,
knock me off this platform.
I'll give you fifteen minutes to do it."

With every minute that went by,
he kept taunting God,
saying "here I am God. I'm still waiting."

About that time
a 300 pound football player,
walking down the hall over heard
what he was saying.

He rushed in there, put his shoulder down,
he knocked that professor
flying off that platform.

The professor got up in a daze and said,
"What in the world did you do that for?"

The player replied,

"God said He was busy, so He sent me."

*****

I heard about this man,

he came up to a Baptist Pastor and he said,

"Sir, my dog has passed away

and I was wondering

if you could come to my house

and have a funeral for him?

The Pastor seemed kind of annoyed

and he said,

"No, I can't do a funeral for a dog."

The man said, "Well that's too bad

cause I was thinking about making a

$5,000 dollar donation

to your church."

The Pastor smiled and said,

"Why didn't you tell me

your dog was Baptist?"

*****

23

I heard about this man.
He was out walking
through the woods with a friend.

And all of a sudden they came upon
this huge grizzly bear.

They froze in their tracks.
And as the bear intently stared them down,
they contemplated what they should do.

The man turned to his friend and said,
"I think we should run."

His friend said, "Are you crazy?

You can't outrun a grizzly bear."

He said, "I know that.

I don't have to outrun him,

I just have to outrun you."

*****

Chapter 3

MINISTERS AND PASTORS

I heard about this minister that died.
He was standing in line at the Pearly Gates
and in front of him was a man
dressed in a loud shirt,
wearing blue jeans and sunglasses.

Saint Peter asked "What's your name sir?"
He said, "My name is Joe Cohen,
taxi cab driver, New York City."

Peter checked his list and handed him
a Gold Staff and a silk robe and said,
"welcome to heaven."

The minister stepped up and said,
"I'm reverend Joseph Snow,
Pastor of Saint Mary's Cathedral."

Peter checked his list and handed him
a cotton robe and a wooden staff.

He said, "hey wait a minute.
That's not fair.
The taxi cab driver got a Gold Staff
and a silk robe.
How could that be?"

Peter said, "Sir, up here we work by results.

When you preached, people slept,
but when he drove, people prayed."

*****

I heard about this minister
that was driving down the road.

He looked down and accidently veered off
and went through a ditch and ended up
crashing into a telephone pole.

The man behind him pulled over
and ran up to him and said,
"Sir, are you okay?"

The minister said, "Yes I'm fine.
The angel of the Lord was with me."

The man shook his head and said,
"You better let him ride with me,
you're about to kill him."

*****

I heard about this minister.
He was up on the pulpit preaching away
one Sunday morning when he noticed a
man on the front row sound asleep.

That made him so aggravated
he started preaching louder and harder,

but it seemed like the louder he got,
the sounder he slept.

So he finally stopped
right in the middle of his sermon
and he said to the man sitting next to him,
"Would you please wake that man up?"

The man said, "Wake him up yourself.
YOU put him to sleep."

*****

I heard about this Pastor.
He decided to skip church one Sunday
morning and go play golf.

He told his assistant he wasn't feeling well.
And he drove to a golf course in another city
where nobody would know him.

He teed off on the first hole and suddenly
the wind picked up his ball and carried it

an extra hundred yards
and blew it right into the hole
for a 420 yard "hole in one."

An angel looked at God and said,
"What did you do that for?"

God smiled and said,
"Who's he gonna tell?"

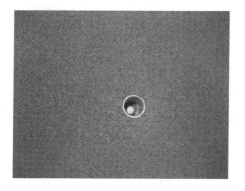

*****

I heard about this Pastor.

He was raising money for a new sanctuary.

He told his congregation
one Sunday morning
"If anybody will give a thousand dollars,
you can pick out the next three hymns."

A little old lady in the back raised up her hand and said, "Pastor, I'll do it."

He was so excited.
He said, "Thank you so much.

Go ahead and pick out
the next three hymns."

She looked over the congregation and said,
"I'll take him
and him
and him."

*****

I heard about this minister
that was out bear hunting.

He searched and searched
all through the woods
but didn't see any sign of a bear.

Finally in frustration he threw his gun down
and went down to the stream to cool off.

About that time he saw this
huge grizzly bear
racing toward him.

He fell on his knees and said,

"Please God protect me.

I'm asking You God

to convert this bear into a Christian."

Miraculously the bear froze in its tracks,

put up both paws toward the heavens

and said,

"Thank You Lord

for this food I'm about to eat."

*****

Chapter 4

<u>MISCELLANEOUS</u>

I heard about this little girl.
She was sitting on her Grandfather's lap
and she noticed how wrinkled his face was.

And as she contemplated the difference
between hers and his, she said,
"Gran Daddy, did God make you?"

He laughed and said,
"Yes honey, God made me a long time ago."

She said, "Well, did God make me?"

He said, "Yes, God made you just a little while ago."

She thought about it a moment and said, "Gran Daddy, God's getting better, isn't he?"

*****

I heard about this
Sunday morning church service.

It was going just fine when all of a sudden
this lightning bolt hit.

And when the smoke cleared
Satan himself was standing
behind the podium.

People panicked and ran out of the building
as fast as they could.

And Satan stood there with glee,
but suddenly his mood changed
when he noticed a woman
sitting on the front row
just as calm as could be.

He said, "Lady, do you know who I am?"
She said, "I sure do."

37

He said, "Aren't you afraid of me?"
She said, "No I'm not."

He said, "Why not?"
She said, "Why should I be?
For 30 years I've been married to your brother."

*****

I heard about this husband and wife...
They'd been arguing and now
they were giving each other
the silent treatment.

The man had to catch a flight
early the next day
and he needed his wife to wake him up
at 5 in the morning.

Not wanting to break the silence,
he wrote a note
and put it on her side of the bed
that said,

38

"Please wake me up at 5."

The next morning he got up at 8.
He missed his flight.

He was so upset he went in to ask
why she didn't wake him up

and he noticed a piece of paper
on his side of the bed.

He opened it up.
It said, "Get up its 5."

*****

I heard about this airplane
that was about to crash.

There were four passengers,
but only three parachutes.

The first passenger said,
"I'm a leading heart surgeon.
My patients need me."

He grabbed the first parachute and jumped.

The second passenger said,
"I'm a rocket scientist.
One of the smartest men in the world
My country needs me."

He took the second parachute and jumped.

The third passenger was Pope John Paul.
He said to the fourth passenger,
a ten year old boy scout,
"Son, I'm old and frail,

you take the last parachute."

The Boy Scout said,
"That's okay sir,
there's still two parachutes left.

The world's smartest man just jumped out
with my backpack."

*****

I heard about this man and his wife.
They argued for months over who should
make the coffee in the morning.

The man definitely thought
it was the wife's job
and she just didn't agree.

After several heated debates
she finally said,
"I can prove from the bible
that it's your job."

He said, "There's nothing in the bible about making coffee.
She said, "Sure there is."

She called him over and opened her bible and pointed to the book of "He-brews".

The End

Here is an EXCERPT from Don's "Joel's Gems – Joel Osteen Quotes"

INTRODUCTION

I have always been attracted to "self help" books, cassettes, authors, videos, you name it and if it is inspirational, motivational or oriented to success in any way, than you can be sure that I'm interested. I'm also a Christian and have always believed that a successful life must be one that has God in it.

Back in the 1980's, due to the type of job I held at a Baltimore printing company where I spent much of my time in a cubicle,

I began listening to a huge amount of audio cassettes by successful authors such as Tony Robbins, Jim Rohn, Earl Nightingale, Zig Ziglar, Norman Vincent Peale, Denis Waitley, Og Mandino and the list goes on. I still have a large collection of those cassette programs today on my bookshelf.

At about that same time, on Sunday mornings I began watching a few preachers on television and I began to notice that there seemed to be a very clear correlation between what the preachers were saying and the principles that were taught by the self help authors that I was listening to daily.

I actually remember telling my wife (Sandy) about it. I felt as though I had discovered something that perhaps no one else had realized (how naïve I was back then, lol). I began to imagine how cool it would be if the two could come together in one person. Do you know what I mean?

I began to wonder... what if either a self help author would show how their teachings were supported scripturally (although they occasionally would reference one or two universal ones, like the golden rule), **OR** if a preacher would emphasize and present examples of success as a result of following God's word.

Well, if you know who Joel Osteen is and didn't just somehow find yourself reading this, than you know where I'm going with this.

Joel Osteen is that person!

I was probably the only one in my circle of friends and relatives that watched television preachers at that time, so of course it was only natural that I was the first to discover him. He became my favorite preacher almost immediately and I started telling others about him and encouraging them to tune in to his broadcasts.

I have now watched him religiously (no pun intended) since his broadcasts first appeared in my area and quite frankly they are one of the highlights of my week. We are all three dimensional beings, physical, mental and spiritual. And as such we must feed all three. Many folks on the planet seem to think that they can be all they can be without feeding their spirits.

I suppose that most people that will read this book will already be Joel Osteen fans and *IF that is you* then we have that in common because in case you haven't noticed already, I AM a BIG Joel Osteen fan. If you've seen him in person or just seen him on TV, then you already know that his messages are positive, inspirational, loving, sincere and at times very funny. And if you expose yourself to his messages long enough and often enough then he'll have you becoming positive too!

Joel has been referred to as "America's Voice of Hope". In publishing this book it is my hope that I can help in some way to spread his message and I can think of no better person that could you choose to learn from or expose yourself to, than Joel Osteen.

I have organized these quotes into groups but I'm sure that you'll see that many of these quotes could just as easily been classified under other groups as well. In my opinion, that's just the nature of quotes. They can be perceived in a different light depending on your frame of mind or what's going on in your life at that time. The first time you read them, some may not seem to mean much and yet at a later time may strike you as exactly what you needed.

It is my hope that you will enjoy reading them at least as much as I do!

Don Pasco

———————————

GRATITUDE

"The seeds of discouragement, cannot take
root in a grateful heart"

****

"If you're not happy today... if you're down
or when you're tempted to get discouraged,
the quickest way out of that is to stop
focusing on what you don't have
and start thanking God
For what you do have."

****

"When we get up in the morning,
before we read the newspaper,
before we turn on the TV,
before we think about our problems,
the first thing we should do is
thank God that we're alive."

****

"You cannot go through the day
negative and depressed
as long as you have a spirit
of thanksgiving in your heart."

****

"We have to realize that every day
is a gift from God.
Once this day is gone,
we can never get it back.
How are you going
to choose to live it?"

****

"If you see somebody living
on the streets;
Pray for them and then learn to say
Father Thank You that I have a home.

If you see somebody in a wheel chair,
Bless them and then say
Father Thank You that I am able to walk.

If you're "IN" a wheel chair
and not able to walk;
Thank God that you can see.

If you don't have legs,
thank God that you have arms.

Find some reason to be grateful.
We can all find some reason
to give thanks, and being grateful
Is the key to living a happy life."

****

"Are you going to go

through the day negative?

Discouraged?

Focused on your problems?

What you _Don't_ have

and _Who_ hurt you?

Get away from that junk and find

some reason to be grateful."

****

I hope that you
have enjoyed this excerpt of
"Joel's Gems – Joel Osteen Quotes"

For information about this or any of
my books, please visit Amazon.com
and search for Don Pasco or visit:
Ebooksworthreading.com

IF YOU ENJOYED THIS BOOK
YOU'RE SURE TO ENJOY THESE
OTHER BEST SELLERS

Recommended Reads

21 Prayers of Gratitude:
**Overcoming Negativity
Through the Power of Prayer
and God's Word (A Life of Gratitude)
*by Shelley Hitz***

Every Day a Friday:
How to Be Happier 7 Days a Week

by Joel Osteen

How to Hear the Voice of God

by Tanya Guerrier

About the Author

Don Pasco was born and raised in Baltimore, Maryland. The 4 things that he is most proud of is his beautiful wife Sandy and their 3 wonderful children, Joe, Jill and Lisa.

Don loves music and played drums (and sang) in a Top 40 band back in the '70s. Today he enjoys karaoke and singing in his Church's choir on Christmas Eve. He is also an avid Ravens (and Orioles) fan and loves sitting on the beach while vacationing in Ocean City Maryland. A strong believer in

Christianity Don enjoys helping others to build their faith and to look for and focus on the good things in life... to realize that we're all connected on some level and it's our responsibility to encourage others to come up higher.

****

One Last Thing

If you enjoyed this book I'd be very grateful if you would post a short review on Amazon. Your support really does make a difference and I read all the reviews personally so I can get your feedback and make my books even better.

If you'd like to leave a review, then all you need to do is return to the site where you made your purchase and search for the title or the author (That's me!) Don Pasco in the search box and click on this book (Joel Osteen Jokes – 2 Book Combo). Or if you made your purchase on Amazon, you can find it on my Amazon Author page at:

EbooksWorthReading.com

Thank you!
Don Pasco

*****

Other Books by Don Pasco

Self help Category

Happy As a Rat in a Trash Can

~ How to Raise Your Happiness Level

Joel's Gems Series

Joel Osteen Quotes

Joel Osteen Quotes Volume 2

~ Inspirational Collections of Joel's Quotes

Joel Osteen Jokes (Original)

Joel Osteen Jokes Volume 2

~ Hilarious Collections of Joel's Jokes

Joel Osteen Quotes & Jokes –

~ Double Combo Pack

Music Quiz Games

Name That Band –

~ The Multiple Choice Music Quiz Game

Name That Artist –

Multiple Choice Music Celebrity Quiz Game

No part of this publication may be copied, reproduced in any format, by any means, electronic or otherwise, without prior consent from the copyright owner and publisher of this book.

Book 2 of 2 Book Combo

JOEL'S GEMS

"Joel Osteen Jokes"

Volume 2

Another Hilarious Collection
Of
Joel Osteen's
Funniest
Short, Clean Jokes

By Don Pasco

http://ebooksworthreading.com

Other books by Don Pasco

"Joyce Meyer Quotes"

Encouraging Words of Faith, Hope And

Instant Inspiration

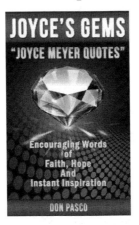

Happy as a Rat in a Trash Can
How to Raise Your Happiness Level

Table of Contents

Free Bonuses

Joel Osteen Jokes Volume 2
(Video version)
Joel Osteen Jokes Volume 2
(Audio version)

For a limited time purchasers of Joel's Gems "Joel Osteen Jokes Volume 2" can receive the audio book version AND the video version of the same title by visiting the page below. So if you would like to watch Joel deliver these jokes in his funny and entertaining way or just listen while doing something else, visit the URL below to claim your bonuses.

donpasco.com/joels-jokes-vol-2-free-bonuses

Introduction

If you are already familiar with Joel's Jokes then you already know that what makes these jokes so cool is because they are short, clean and funny!

If you like to tell jokes yourself, you can use these in almost any scenario, without fear that any are "low class" (for lack of a better term).

Sure you may have heard a few of these before, but that doesn't mean that they aren't funny second time around. Does it?

Every week Pastor Joel Osteen likes to get started with something funny. Having a sense of humor is an important attribute for all of us to have. We all need the capacity to laugh. After all, **joy is a gift from God.**

We all know there's more than enough negative things in the world that we hear about each and every day, either through the news media or even in our own lives and the lives of those around us.

Are You a Light Hearted Person?

I personally feel that we should always be looking for things that make us laugh. I like the feeling of being a "Light Hearted" person and I hope you do too.

And if you're anything like me, you'll enjoy telling these jokes just as much as reading them.

Joel states upfront that the jokes are not doctrinally correct... that they're just to make us laugh so I too want to mention that here.

Are you ready to get started?

Well then turn the page and get your giggle going.

I heard about this new police recruit

I heard about this new police recruit.
He was taking his final exam.
He was in the front of this big classroom
and the Sergeant asked him,
"What would you do if you had to arrest
your own Mother-in-law?"
Without missing a beat he said, "Call for
backup."

*****

I heard about this man

I heard about this man that was in a dark
restaurant. He leaned over to the woman
next to him and said, "Hey, would you like
to hear a blonde joke?"

She said, "well before you tell me, you should know that I am blonde,
6 feet tall and a professional body builder.

And the lady next to me is blonde,
6 foot two and a professional wrestler.

And the lady next to her is blonde,
6 foot five and the kick-boxing champion of the world.

Now, do you still want to tell me the blonde joke?

He thought about it a moment and said,

"No, not if I'm going to have to explain it 3 times.

*****

I heard about this wealthy man

I heard about this wealthy man
that was known for being eccentric.

He was having a big party at his house
and in his backyard he had a huge pool
filled with alligators and sharks.

He said to the guests,
"Anyone that will swim across my pool
I'll give you anything you want."

In a few minutes there was a big splash
and a man was in there going 90 to
nothing... dodging alligators, maneuvering
around the sharks.

He made it to the other side just in the nick
of time and got out as frantic as can be.

The wealthy man said,

"I can't believe that you're the bravest
person I've ever met.

Now what is it that you would want?"

The man said, "What I want, more than
anything else is the name of the person
that pushed me in."

*****

I heard about this lady

I heard about this lady that died
and she found herself standing
at the pearly gates.

Saint Peter said, "You can't come in unless
you correctly spell a word."

She said, "What word?"
He said "any word."
So she spelled the word love. L-O-V-E

Peter said, "Welcome to heaven."
Then Peter asked her if she would
take his place.
He instructed her, "if anybody comes
just follow the same procedure."

Well, in a few minutes this lady sees
her ex-husband coming up.

She said, "What are you doing here?"

He said, "I just had a heart attack.

Did I really make it to heaven?"

She said, "Not yet.

You have to correctly spell a word."

He said, "What word?"

After a long pause she said Czechoslovakia.

*****

I heard about these 2 little boys

I heard about these 2 little boys.
They were spending the night
with their grandparents.

Before they went to bed
they got down on their knees
to say their prayers.

The youngest one started praying
at the top of his lungs,
saying, "God, I pray that you'll
give me a new bicycle
and I pray that you'll
give me a new playstation
and I pray that you'll
give me a new DVD."

His brother said "why are you screaming?
God is not deaf."

The little boy said, "I know that,
but Grandmother is."

*****

I heard about this groom

I heard about this groom.
During the wedding rehearsal
he said to the Pastor,
"I'll make a deal with ya.

If you'll change my wedding vows
and leave out all of the
Love, Honor and Obey stuff,
I'll give you a hundred dollars."

He pressed the hundred dollars into the
Ministers hands and he walked away
with a smile.

The next day during the ceremony the
minister said,

"Do you promise to
bow down before your wife...
to take her breakfast in bed every day...
to fulfill her every wish?"

He gulped in astonishment.
Finally in a weak voice he said, "I do."

And then he leaned forward and said,
"Hey, I thought we had a deal?"

The minister handed him his money back
and said,
"Your wife made me a much better offer."

*****

I heard about this Archaeologist

I heard about this Archaeologist
from New York.
He dug down 10 feet
and found traces of copper wiring
dating back a hundred years.
He concluded that New Yorkers
had a telephone network
over a hundred years ago.

Not to be outdone,
an Archaeologist from California
dug down 20 feet
and found copper wiring
dating back 200 hundred years.
He concluded that Californians
had a massive communications network
a hundred years BEFORE the New Yorkers.

Hearing these reports, Bubba from Texas

dug down 30 feet on his farm

and found absolutely nothing.

He concluded 300 years ago

Texans had already gone wireless.

*****

I heard about this minister

I heard about this minister
that was out walking down the street
and he came upon this group of young boys
that were surrounding a little dog.

He asked them what they were doing
and they explained
that they were having a contest
and whoever could tell the biggest lie,
would get to keep the dog.

The minister launched into
a ten minute sermon on lying,
beginning with
"don't you know that lying is a sin?
and ending with
"When I was your age I never told a lie."

There was complete silence.

And just when he thought

he'd gotten through to them,

the youngest boy spoke up and said,

"alright, give 'em the dog."

*****

I heard about this little girl

I heard about this little girl
She asked her Mother
how the human race got started?

The Mother explained
how God made Adam and Eve
and they had children and on and on and
here we are today.

A few days later she asked her Father
the same question.
He explained how many years ago
there were monkeys.
Little by little they became more like people
and now here we are.

Confused she went back to her Mom
and said,

"Mom, you said God created people.
Dad said we came from monkeys.
How can that be?"

She said, "Oh honey, that's easy.
I told you about my side of the family.
Dad told you about his."

*****

I heard about this man

I heard about this man.
He was walking up to a country store
and there was a little boy
sitting on the front porch
with a HUGE dog sitting next to him.

The man said, "Son, does your dog bite?"
He said, "no sir, my dog doesn't bite."
The man reached down to pet the dog
and the dog took about half of his arm off.

He pulled it back and said,
"son, I thought you said
your dog didn't bite?"
The little boy said,
"That's not my dog."

*****

I heard about this southern baptist man

I heard about this southern baptist man
named Bill.
He loved to sneak off
to the horse races and bet.
And one day after losing
almost all of his money,
he noticed a priest step down on the track
and bless a horse.

Sure enough, the horse won first place.
The next race,
the priest blessed another horse.
Once again, that horse won.

So Bill went to the ATM machine
and took out all of his money.
This time the priest not only
touched the horse's forehead,
but his eyes, his ears and all of his hoofs.

Feeling confident, Bill bet all of his money,
but right in the middle of the race
the horse fell over and died.

Bill could NOT believe it.
He went over to the priest and said,
"What in the world happened?"

The priest said,
"That's the problem with you Protestants,
you don't know the difference
between a blessing and the Last Rites."

*****

I heard about this middle aged woman

I heard about this middle aged woman.
She had a heart attack
and on the operating table
she asked God if this was it?

God said, "No, you have 40 more years."
Upon recovery she decided to stay in the
hospital and have a facelift, a tummy tuck,
liposuction, an extreme makeover.

Two months later
as she was leaving the hospital
she was hit by a car and killed.

She got to heaven and said,
"God, I thought you said I had
40 more years?"

God said, I'm sorry.
I didn't recognize you."

*****

I heard about these 3 sons

I heard about these 3 sons that left home
and went out and prospered.

One day they got back together
to discuss the gifts that they bought
their elderly Mother.

The first son said,
"I built Mother a big house."
The second son said,
"I got her a fancy car."
The third one said,
"Since I know how much Mother
loves to read the bible,
but she can barely see now,
I got her a specially trained parrot
that can quote the entire bible."

In a few days, they got a letter from their
Mother, it said,

"Milton, the house you built me
is way too big.
Jerold, the car you bought me
is way too small,
but my dearest Donald,
your simple gift, is my favorite.

The chicken was delicious."

*****

I heard about this guy

I heard about this guy.
He was late to work for the
3rd day in a row.

His boss said sarcastically,
"okay, what's your excuse this time."

He said, "I'm so sorry but my wife
asked to drive me to work.
And I told her she didn't need to,
but she insisted and said she could be
ready in 10 minutes.

But then when we left
the drawbridge was up
and I had to swim across the river,
fighting off alligators,
then a helicopter picked me up,
put me on top of a building,
I ran down 60 flights of stairs

and got here as quickly as I could."

His boss shook his head and said,
"You expect me to believe that?

No woman can get dressed
in just 10 minutes."

*****

I heard about this man (on vacation)

I heard about this man.
He was on vacation in Jerusalem
with his family.

All of a sudden his Mother in law died.
He went to make arrangements
to get her body back home
and the Consulate said it would cost
$5000 dollars to have her shipped
and $150 dollars to have her buried
right there in Jerusalem.

After deep thought he told the consulate he
wanted to have her body shipped.

The consulate said, "Well boy,
you must of really loved
your Mother-in-law?"

He said, "No, it's not so much that.

I just remember a case here many years ago

where they buried somebody

and on the 3rd day He arose.

I can't take that chance."

*****

I heard about this 85 year old man

I heard about this 85 year old man.
He was out fishing one day
and he heard this voice saying
"pick me up".

He looked all around
and didn't see anything
and he thought he was dreaming.

Then he heard it again.
"Pick Me Up".

He looked down
and saw a frog on the ground.

He said in amazement,
"are you talking to me?"

The frog said, "Yes, pick me up and kiss me
and I'll turn into a beautiful bride."

He quickly picked the frog up
and put him in his front pocket.

The frog said, "Hey!
What are you doing?
I said kiss me
and I'll turn into a beautiful bride."

The man said, "No thanks.
At my age, I'd rather have a talking frog."

*****

I heard about this elderly couple

I heard about this elderly couple
that had been married for over 60 years.

They were at a church fellowship
and someone asked them
the secret of their success.

The man told how he always treated his wife
with respect and he took her on trips all
over the world.

He said, "In fact, for our 25th wedding
anniversary I took her to Beijing China."

Everyone kinda clapped.

Someone spoke up and said

"Whatcha you do for your

50th wedding anniversary?"

He said, "I went back and picked her up."

*****

I heard about this little 3 year old boy

I heard about this little 3 year old boy.
He had a sore throat.
His Mom took him to the Doctor
and the Doctor put his stethoscope on his
chest to listen to his lungs
and he said to the little boy,
"Okay, just be still buddy.

I'm just going to check
to see if Barney's in here.

The little boy said, "Jesus is in my heart,
but Barney's on my underwear."

*****

I heard about this reporter

I heard about this reporter.
He was visiting churches
all across the nation.

While in New York he noticed this golden
phone on the wall with a sign that said
"Calls ~ $10,000 dollars per minute".

He asked the Pastor what it meant
and the Pastor explained how that was
a direct line to Heaven.

If you were willing to pay the price,
you could talk directly to God.

The reporter continued visiting other
churches and encountered the same golden
phone with the same sign.

When he finally made it down to Texas,

he saw the phone on the wall

but the sign said

25 cents per call

Intrigued he asked the Pastor why

it was so much cheaper?

The Pastor said, "You're in Texas.

Now it's a local call."

*****

I heard about this man

I heard about this man.
Somebody had stolen his wife's credit card.

A couple of months later
the company called him and said,
"Sir, we have good news.
We found the credit card."

Without missing a beat he said,
"Tell the thief to keep it.
He spends less than my wife."

*****

I heard about this husband

I heard about this husband that died.
He left his wife $20,000 dollars.

After the funeral, his wife told a friend
that she was totally broke.

The friend said,
"What do you mean you're broke?
I thought you had $20,000 dollars.

She said, "Well, I spent $5000 dollars
on the funeral and $15,000 on the
memorial stone."

The friend said, "Wow, that was some stone.
How big was it?"

She held up her finger and said,
"3 and a half carats."

*****

I heard about these 3 men

I heard about these 3 men
that were traveling together,
a Hindu Priest, a Jewish Rabbi
and a Televangelist.

They stopped at a farm house for lodging
and the farmer said,
"I only have room for 2 in the house.
Someone's going to have to stay
in the barn."

The Hindu Priest said, "I'll do it."
After a few minutes
there was a knock on the door.

He said "I can't stay out there.
There's a cow, and cows are sacred
in our religion."

The Jewish Rabbi said, "I'll do it."

After a few minutes,

there was a knock on the door.

He said, "I can't stay out there.

There's a pig and that wouldn't be Kosher."

The Televangelist finally said,

"Alright, I'll do it."

In a few minutes

there was a knock on the door.

It was the cow and the pig.

*****

I heard about this Christian woman

I heard about this Christian woman
that was on an airplane reading her bible.

The man next to her said,
"You don't believe all that stuff in there,
do you?"

She said, "Of course I do, it's the bible."

He said, "Well what about that guy
that was swallowed by the whale?"

She said, "You mean Jonah?
Yes I believe that too."

He said, "How could he possibly survive
all that time inside a whale?"

She thought about it for a moment
and said, "I don't know.
When I get to Heaven I'll have to ask him."

He said sarcastically,
"Well what if he's not in Heaven?"

She smiled and said,
"Then you're gonna have to ask him."

*****

This one was sent to me by a woman

I like to start with
something funny each week...
I'll preface this by saying
this was sent to me by a woman.

According to the Alaska department
of fish and game, while both male and
female reindeer grow antlers in the summer
each year, male reindeer drop their antlers
at the beginning of winter, in late
November.

Female reindeer however,
maintain their antlers until the spring.

Therefore all of Santa's reindeer from Rudolf
to Blitzen had to be female.

We should have known.

Only women would be able to drag around
a fat man in a red velvet suit
all around the world in one night
and not get lost.

I don't know what to say (chuckling).
No comment. Chuckling again

*****

I heard about these 3 men

I heard about these 3 men.
A Baptist, a Catholic and a Charismatic
suddenly died and went to Heaven.

Upon arrival Saint Peter said,
"I'm so sorry but your living quarters
are not quite ready."

He didn't know what to do with them.
Finally he decided to call the devil and ask
him if he would keep them for a couple of
days.

Satan reluctantly agreed.
A few hours later Satan called back and
said, "You've got to come get these guys.

The Catholic man is forgiving everybody,
the Baptist is saving everybody
and the Charismatic has already raised
enough money for air conditioning.

*****

I heard about this blonde lady

I heard about this blonde lady...
and you know I'm married to a beautiful,
smart, intelligent blonde.

This is just a joke.
But this blonde was at Target
and she saw this thermos up on the shelf.

She asked the clerk what it was.
He said, "That's a thermos.
You've never used one of those?"

She said, "No. What does it do."

He said, "It keeps things hot and it keeps
things cold."

The next day she showed up at work with it.

Her boss said, "I've never seen YOU with a thermos.

What do you have in there?"
She said, "Two popsicles and some coffee."

****

I heard about this Pastor

I heard about this Pastor that was in the
lobby after the service greeting people.

He saw a man that he hadn't seen
in a long, long time.

He pulled him over to the side and said,
"Sir, you need to join the army of the Lord."

He said, "What do you mean?
I'm in the army of the Lord.

"The Pastor said, "Well, how come I only see
you on Christmas and Easter?"

The man whispered back,

"because I'm in the Secret Service."

****

I heard about these 3 people

I heard about these 3 people
a Russian, an American and a Blonde.

They were talking one day.
The Russian proudly said,
"We were the first ones in space."

The American said,
"Well we were the first ones on the moon."

The Blonde said, "That's nothin'.
We're going to be the first ones on the Sun."

The Russian and the American,
they laughed and said,
"What are you talkin' about?

You can't go to the Sun.
It's too hot. You'll burn up."

The Blonde said, "We're not that dumb. We're going to go at night."

I heard about this man (at the airport)

I heard about this man that was at the
airline ticket counter, hollering and
screaming at the agent... being so rude.

As he continued to rant and rave
the agent was just as calm and polite as
could be.

She treated him so respectfully,
like it didn't even bother her.

He left and the next man stepped up
and said, "Wow! I am so impressed.
You must be a Christian.

How could you possibly be so kind to him?"
She smiled and said,
"Aww, it wasn't that hard.

See, he's going to Detroit,

but his bags are going to Bangkok."

****

I heard about these 3 sisters

I heard about these 3 sisters
that all lived together.

They were ages 96, 94 and 92.

One day the 96 year old draws a bath
and she puts one foot in and she pauses.

She hollers downstairs,
"I can't remember if I was getting in,
or getting out."

The 94 year old says, "I don't know.
I'll come up there to see."

And she gets half way up the stairs
and she pauses and says,
"I can't remember if I was going up
or coming down."

The 92 year old shook her head and said,
"Man, I hope I never get that forgetful."
And she knocked on wood for good luck.

And then she said, "Hang on,
I'll come help both of you
as soon as I see who's at the door."

The End

For your enjoyment we have included
an <u>EXCERPT</u> from Don's book

"Happy As a Rat in a Trash Can"

**No it's NOT a children's book
as you'll see below**

Happy As a Rat
in a Trash Can

How to Raise Your Happiness Level

By Don Pasco

donpasco.com

www.amazon.com/author/don-pasco

INTRODUCTION

Only 1 life that soon will pass…
Only what's done with love will last

Many years ago I saw a drawing of an elephant with 5 men who were all blindfolded. Each of the blindfolded men were experiencing the elephant in a different way.

- One was sitting on top of it.
- Another was holding the elephant's tail.
- One was holding the elephant's trunk
- while another was hugging the elephant's leg,
- And the 5th was grasping the elephant's ear.

I don't recall whether or not there was a caption that went along with the drawing, but I was strongly impacted by the message it conveyed. It was obvious that each of those men, if asked to describe the elephant, would have completely different opinions.

That drawing still sticks in my mind today and reminds me that we all see things differently, even though we may be experiencing the exact same thing.

If you will let this image impact you the way it did me, you can become a more understanding person of people and situations in *your* life. You can become a little more tolerant of things you don't understand, because you will know that there is always more to every situation than meets the eye.

Our Senses Are Limited

Also, it's important to realize that as wonderful as it is to have our 5 senses, they are limited.

Just for example purposes, let's talk about our hearing. Most of us know that dogs and cats can hear things that we humans cannot.

According to Wikipedia:

The range of human hearing is typically considered to be between 20 Hz and 18 kHz.

The top end of a dog's hearing range is about 45 kHz, while a cat's is 64 kHz

http://en.wikipedia.org/wiki/Dog_whistle

Keep this thought in mind when we get to the section on faith.

Perhaps it is why the bible tells us to:

"walk by faith; not by sight."
2 Corinthians 5:7

Happiness - A Universal Desire

What is happiness and why do we want it?

According to dictionary.com happiness is:
1. the quality or state of being happy.
2. good fortune; pleasure; contentment; joy.

Do you agree with this definition? It's not bad, is it? But there's so much more that we could add to it. Don't you think?

On a scale of 1 to 10, with 1 being not happy at all and 10 being very, very happy, how happy would you say you are right now, BEFORE reading this book?

Now remember that number. Perhaps you could write it down somewhere. Let's see if we can work together to raise it up just like a student would work to raise up his school grades.

I'm going to give you some ideas. You can take them... or leave them, but I hope you'll at least give them all a fair chance.

Without giving away my exact age, as of the time of this writing I have been on the planet for over half a century. Since I don't know you personally, I may be old enough to be your father, or young enough to be your son, but I trust you'll agree that that would be enough time to gain at least a little wisdom. Of course, you'll have to be the judge of that as you read through the book.

One of my primary goals in writing this book is to pass at least some of that wisdom on to you through the words on these pages. Please understand that I am NOT saying that I am smarter or more intelligent than you or any other person that has or will ever read this book. Just as each of the blindfolded men have information not shared by the other four, it's the same with you and me.

In fact, I want you to know upfront that although I've been on this planet for over half a century,

There is really <u>only one thing</u> I know "for sure"...

And that is...

I DON'T KNOW ANYTHING "FOR SURE"

That may sound like an amusing statement and it is, but... it is also a truthful statement. There have been times in my life when I sincerely felt that I was absolutely certain about a particular thing... and then later found out that I was either dead wrong or did not have all of the pertinent information which led to my incorrect conclusion(s). There have been times when I have misinterpreted my source, and there have been times when my source was incorrect, even though they thought they were being truthful. I suspect this may have also happened to you (or will at some point in your future). And let's not forget what I just mentioned above about our limited senses. They too may contribute to our errors in judgment.

In this book, I talk about some of my own personal experiences, but I will also be referencing things I've read in other books or heard on audio books by some of the greatest authors of our time.

But mostly it will be about things that I've noticed that I've not heard very often (if at all) that seem like common sense, yet could be very helpful if people would think about it in the same way that I do. I often find myself thinking "Am I the only one who thinks like this?" and when I point these things out to others, they are quick to agree that they make perfect sense.

I firmly believe that these things can and will help you if you will adopt them, but...

First... I Need to Gain Your Trust

If this book is really going to help you the way I intend it to, then the first thing I need to do is gain your trust.

Most of you who are reading this book will not know me, so I need to make a connection with you... I need to relate to you in some way so that you can get a sense of who I am. You will need to decide if I am a credible source, and whether or not I am worthy of your time and attention.

How Will I Do That?

The only way that I can do that is by holding your attention long enough to make some interesting points that accomplish those things. Otherwise, I will lose you and you will go on with your life and forget all about this book. And that would be a shame. I am hopeful that this will be one of those "keeper" books. You know, one that you will treasure and keep. One that you will always want to know is available to read or reread any time you want.

What I Ask of You

If you will commit to reading at least two chapters, I feel very strongly that *I will* gain your trust... that *you will* get a sense of who I am... that you will decide that I am a credible source and that at the end of this book, you will be glad that you gave me a chance to serve you.

Although I will need to make that connection by letting you gain an understanding of who I am, *this book is __not__ about me*. **It is about you**. It is about you becoming a little more faithful, a little more grateful, a little more understanding, a little more forgiving, a little more thoughtful, a little more caring, and a little more loving.

Why?

Because these are the things that beget happiness.

What I intend to do in this book is share some thoughts and ideas that could possibly help you to see things a little bit differently than you do now. And if I succeed, I'm sure you'll be as Happy as a rat in a trash can!

"Change the way you look at things and the things you look at change."

Dr. Wayne W. Dyer

———

Get wisdom, get understanding;
do not forget my words or turn away from them.
Proverbs 4: 5

Let's get started!

I hope that you have enjoyed
this excerpt from Don's

"Happy As a Rat in a Trash Can"

For information about this or any of
Don's books, please visit Amazon.com
and search for Don Pasco or visit:
Ebooksworthreading.com

Recommended Reading

21 Prayers of Gratitude:
**Overcoming Negativity
Through the Power of Prayer
and God's Word (A Life of Gratitude)**
by Shelley Hitz

Every Day a Friday:
How to Be Happier 7 Days a Week

by Joel Osteen

How to Hear the Voice of God

by Tanya Guerrier

About the Author

Don Pasco spent 26 years at a Baltimore Printing company before his printing career ended in 2003 when the company closed the plant.

Believing that everything happens for a reason, Don was excited about the possibilities his future held.

Today, Don loves working from home as an author, publisher and internet marketer.

He is a huge Joel Osteen fan and also enjoys rooting for his hometown Baltimore Ravens and Baltimore Orioles. He loves vacationing in Ocean City Maryland and cruising with his wife Sandy.

He is a strong believer in Christianity and enjoys helping others to build their faith in the Lord and encouraging them to recognize the blessings and talents God has bestowed upon us all.

If you would like to receive a FREE series of Joel Osteen Quotes personally selected by Don sent directly to your inbox just go to: http://BestJoelOsteenQuotes.com/Likes/InspirationalQuotes and tell us where to send them and you will start receiving them instantly!"

You're not defined by your past; you're prepared by it. You may have encountered some great obstacles, but it's because God has a great future in front of you.
Joel Osteen

One Last Thing

If you enjoyed this book I'd be very grateful if you'd post a short review on Amazon. Your support really does make a difference and I read all the reviews personally so I can get your feedback and make my books even better.

If you'd like to leave a review then please go to Amazon.com and search for Don Pasco in the search box. Then click on this book or you can find it on my Amazon Author page at:

EbooksWorthReading.com

Thank you!

Don Pasco

*****

Other Books by Don Pasco

Self help Category

Happy As a Rat in a Trash Can

~ How to Raise Your Happiness Level

Joel's Gems Series

Joel Osteen Quotes

Joel Osteen Quotes Volume 2

~ Inspirational Collections of Joel's Quotes

Joel Osteen Jokes

~ Hilarious Collections of Joel's Jokes

Joel Osteen Jokes Volume 2 (this book)

Joel Osteen Quotes & Jokes –

~ Double Combo Pack

Music Quiz Games

Name That Band –

~ The Multiple Choice Music Quiz Game

Name That Artist –

Multiple Choice Music Celebrity Quiz Game

No part of this publication may be copied, reproduced in any format, by any means, electronic or otherwise, without prior consent from the copyright owner and publisher of this book.